SOIE SAUVAGE

SOIE SAUVAGE

poems by

OLGA BROUMAS

COPPER CANYON PRESS

Thanks to the editors of Lady-Unique-Inclination-of-the-
Night, Northwest Review, 13th Moon, and Trellis,
where some of these poems first appeared.
The author thanks the Oregon Arts Commission and
the National Endowment for the Arts for their support.

Copper Canyon Press
Box 271, Port Townsend, Washington 98368

CONTENTS

for
Deborah Haynes
&
Gary Snyder

OREGON LANDSCAPE WITH LOST LOVER

I take my bike
and ride down to the river
and put my feet into the water
and watch the ten toes play distortions

with the light. I had forgotten all this time
how good it is to sit by water
in sun all day and never have to leave
the river moving

as no lover ever moved
widehipped deadsure and delicate—
after a while I cannot bear
to look. Pleasure dilates me

open as a trellis
free of its green sharp glossy leaves like tongues
made out of mirrors gossiping
in the sun the wind. By which

I mean
somehow
free of the self.
Through all the hungry-eyed

criss-crossing slits along the trellis
finding them leaving them
bare and clean the widehipped delicate
green river flows

voluptuous as any lover anywhere
has been

FIVE INTERIOR LANDSCAPES

for Stephen

I
It's all right. Things slow down. Some light
shines in the convex mirror. The candle burns.
Someone dictates a poem. The blue
field of the sheet live with wiggling
poppies, lashing their sperm-tail stems.
The special sheet, bought for the double
bed of the sleeping loft, four pillows
at its head and feet. Here
one pillow's enough. Inside the sleeping
bag, red afghan
keeps my feverish body not only warm
but dry. I'm not prepared for this. How much
I miss you.

II
The pressure falls sometimes so low
in my veins I can't breathe hard enough
to force the double
vocal cords and call. Next room a woman
friend respects my closed door. Like me
and unlike me, is silent. Right side, arm, thigh
shake for an hour in what Leah who massages me
at home calls
fear. But shaking from the central
muscle to the long thin bone, it puts
more fear in me than it lets go. Not only suffering
but that no one knows
how I suffer. I've found
thermometers are useful props
for saying no to calls from poets' parties. It lies

by the bed like a dictated song. Later I write
or try to write
from life.

III
Still they decide to have a party.
I do not recognize this life. Drinking and drinking
in noisy halls full of smoke for pleasure. The noise
finds me staring wall to wall, alone, a stranger
to my home-brought treasures.   Blue
flowered sheet, red afghan, mirror
shining its scooped-out face. It's all
right. The candle burns. Epiphanies
are only numinous
cliches. Something you've known
the words to all your life undone by Nina
Simone, voice and piano. Be grateful. Stockpile.
Fastidiously, keep your body clean. Live
like a poet you'll write
like one.

IV
Baths, showers, water. The padded
well-soaped scrub. Clean hair. Warm water.
Two years since we went
our ways, over and over I
turn to the ample tub, the glass
stall waterfall, the friendly fixtures.
On the road or camping I crave them
like a fix. I remember my life
the way a tourist
back from a Mediterranean
country remembers. I wash and wash. Nothing sloughs
off, nothing cleans windshields, the rear
view. When I shake I remind myself

it always stops, stay quiet, promise
the worn-out limbs
a bath. If someone dictates a poem you have not seen
before, can it seem
a familiar poem?

V
Strange as it is, the only thing familiar is this act.
Writing. Getting stoned
with anyone since you is bringing home
total strangers. I thought grass cleared
everyone's daily defensive
fog, brought on its kind
of music. The extra gesture. The flower, the odd
piece of silver beside the bowl. Most often now
I like to smoke alone. I try to care
at least as well
for me as I did for you. I didn't know about
such subtle losses. A light pain
that goes on too long gets
forgotten, becomes an agent, you trust
the familiar face till she flashes
a badge and it's you
in the funhouse mirror. In line for lunch, a woman's
voice above the clatter and starch, "It has
to grow a scab before you scratch it."

SWEEPING THE GARDEN

for Deborah Haynes
Slowly learning again to love
ourselves working. Paul Eluard

said the body
is that part of the soul
perceptible by the five senses. To love
the body to love its work
to love the hand that praises both to praise
the body and to love the soul
that dreams and wakes us back alive
against the slothful odds: fatigue
depression loneliness
the perishable still recognition
what needs

be done. *Sweep the garden, any size*
said the roshi. Sweeping sweeping

alone as the garden grows
large or small. Any song
sung working the garden brings
up from sand gravel soil through
straw bamboo wood and less
tangible elements Power
song for the hands Healing
song for the senses what can
and cannot be perceived
of the soul.

WOMAN WITH CHILD

Sucking the acid
from the disk between my teeth
I plunge to find you child
bewildered in the deep
hallucination
where nameless unspoken
you exist intact before you clenched
your kiss a stubborn mouthful
in your pelvic lip. Ritual

suicide at your parents'
knee. In pinafore
and frilly briefs
atop a table rhyming
precosciously by heart *Child*
Bride at twelve I was you mime
a swollen belly *thirteen sons*
and by my husband
only. The audience your parents'

friends laugh
clap and reach for you child
bride body
heat resinous disturbing as you shy
back trip show the lacy
frills. First standing
ovation. You were three. Applause
applause after that act
until you back
hand curtsy. Lifted
from the table thumbs
stray to your nipples lips
stray to your lips they kiss

touch fondle pass you round —arouse
without acknowledging
your passion or the fear
that swells you wordless as a lump
in a throat choked
off. You lose
control. One of them
spanks you. *Without your will*
In pain   Through fear the motifs
of your fantasies unravelling already
down thirty years of garden paths
more balls of wool than you can
track back crossed
eyes like pinballs. Small

childbride mother of
myself small hyperactive
lost in a gaslight labyrinth
trust me I bring the kiss
of a desire like
Demeter's her
daughter tricked by pomegranate
seeds. She bit
the clit-like fruit and forfeited
her sex half-live
an underworld
paraplegic. Post-op your eyes

still crossed
you learned about the body
of a god that seen would blind
you light ripping through
the cortical
powerhouse and its dependent
grists. You imagined your spine

alive exploding
vision like mercury
down from the bulbous
matter of the brain. You longed for that
final ovation
of light the brain consuming
itself in understanding and having
understood burned
obsolete. Little one little unborn

child truth is
your body invisible
till now live sensuous
with its reflex kiss. Open your mouth I
love you give
back the bruised flesh
seed. You do. We touch
it trembling with exhaustion
weak. Truth trust
the weakness
of the body. In darkness

now I spit the disk
of acid climb
stairs down
to kitchen un-
familiar instruments
of food and light. Manage the gas
a ring of fire. Take off clothes shoes tampax clean
our body cold
winter water from the tap three Abyssinian
cats underfoot. Finish the washing. Feel
the slow rivulet on thigh
our blood. Small child I

promise: no more flesh
to chew to touch
the tongue to flesh to pleasure
only chose the few
who know and love the way inside
the labyrinth our body
rocking with relief still
weak by the innocent
gaslight burner. Paper mache
and Christmas-lit across the street a child
bride Mary leans towards a manger.
Fire-warmed fogging on
the pane I sit till dawn

breaks child
I have delivered
through the longest
night. Winter Solstice.

Staten Island, 1977

FOREIGNER

House
Two floors
Down is stove
Down is bath kitchen music
Down is stove and the stack of logs
Up is bed and the climate the tropical
Down is desk next to stove
Around and around floors windows uncurtained
Outside is snow
Unmarked northern profound white snow
Up small woman alone
Icicles
Naked

LANDSCAPE WITH LEAVES AND FIGURE

Passionate Love is Temporary
Insanity the Chinese
say that day
I walked nine miles in the bowl
the hill makes coming round
and round avoiding
the road in
sane I realized a whole
week later at the time
I sank my crepe
soles in the spread
of leaves grass needles
bedding down the path
I took describing
every tree bush fern each
stone leaf stick
isolate
detail in the mind
one woman/it was icy cold/my nose
froze in the air lichen were dancing
up hundred-footed trees the ivy
dirndling up like glitter
flint I stood
there planted
firmly and I could not feel
the cold
wind rain the ivy glinting
savagely like mirrors on the skirts
the six-armed goddess dancing
a storm/wet/it was wet inside
the forest though no rain
was falling it was
sliding

down and you
meanwhile clear
cross-country from the snow
packs of Vermont two weeks one half
a honeydew papaya moon
were eating
while I rimmed the bowl
the woods make in the penetrating
silence between rains in
Oregon in
sane I realized a whole
week later and I said
since you had not yet
left Because
I love you Yes
you said I know that
day

LANDSCAPE WITH POETS

Leaning
over the footbridge the Willamette
River in thaw you said John Berryman
jumped off a bridge like this your
officemate was there he waved
back thinking *friendly*
fellow John
hand raised still
smiling stradled the rail broke
ice

Below
us water hungry
current so swollen it appeared
intimate inflamed

We looked down
river down to sea
so long I held you feeling
a stranger surfacing than fear an ancient species
decimated in the wild wild singing
its last migration down through ice
floes huge emotional the killer
whale the heart

LANDSCAPE WITH NEXT OF KIN

Imagine father that you had a brother were
not an orphan singly that you had a twin
who moved away when he got married had
a kid a similar career whom you had not seen
but heard from frequently for thirty years
imagine meeting him some evening somewhere
familiar to you both not in the village but by
the sea / perhaps / you have

been talking for hours
and for many days
at ease in the proprietor's
gaze — he is young you are old he could have been
a soldier in your regiment that northern province
not so long ago / perhaps he is / you are

here this evening you and your brother seated at the damp
alloy table rusting in some seaside
Patra of the mind identical sighting
the prow of the ferry from Brindisi / perhaps / a woman

bows out from the throng
of tourists very feminine and very strong
resemblance to this man your brother you have never
married / yourself / tonight
are you sipping

the weak milk of your ouzo
having heard everything / at ease / on the other side
of the customs waiting for his daughter your
first blood kin is there anything
in the love you feel

swimming towards him as you did
nine months one heartbeat

pounding like an engine in those waters / is
there anything you won't forgive
her / him

LANDSCAPE WITH DRIVER

for Stephen Bangs

I had my tubes tied on the coast
road to Astoria today it was chilling
driving the weather windy and the sea bright
grey I was alone in the car I was thinking again
I say yes believing you will not harm me having no cause
to believe such things I thought I was being
brave the sea hissed openly the road threw
curves you were back with your father
extending the hearth palm-sized
pebbles in your hands a dull
like your language
weapon

I drove towards the center
for battered women to read my work *believing*
you will not harm me having no cause no part
of that work I had no bruises I kept on
driving hugging
myself around the wheel and driving faster forcing
my attention to the road you were the only
man I made exceptions for believing wanting
to believe we still
could cleave to each other married soul
on soul sloughing our politic
bodies

BANNER

International Women's Day I hitch
myself up by the river to the mountains slowly leaving
spring behind and driving into winter
seven hours mist light rain
light snow low light
finally on the windows all
day the sound was either car
or rain or forest then the rustling
metal click and zipper sleeping
bag the tent the quiet then
no human
voice all day I didn't
speak I hadn't sung was glad the stars
did not come out again like eyes it grew too cold
for snow to fall the snow was all
around soon it took over
my whole attention skin and bones
and brain and blood attendant to its duty
the heart pumped loudly I was so
excited I could feel
deeply again and did feel
summoned surrendered to the land
scape slept at last immersed unlimited
in silence hibernating
animals know how
the nerves relax exhaustively
like this before the final thaw

LENTEN

Still weeks before the equinox
in March strange pleasure
to prepare to come
to visit you in April April
fourteen strange pleasure not to miss you how
different pleasurable this time
immersed in the collective
memorizing of my senses all
fierce all entangled preparations
constantly at the terminals
at the other stations
in the imaginary the mercurial in dreams
the long lope of a mind
uninterrupted like a raga
drone horizon note against which rivers
mountains miles of landscape and the present
sing

ROADSIDE

Old fir young fir
afternoon indiscriminate
cloudy hard to time
stop the car on dirt
road stretch head
towards the sound of river
oblivious still from the high
way speed sweet sound of river
incessant rising through my ears
eyes I'm clear
across the clearing
before I know the wind
is rising in the branches
not the river very cold
wind very dry
no grass or undergrowth
young pine sparse between old pine
dead branches
all the way across
a path I had been crushing
riblike winter-polished twigs
bone dry

BLOCKADE

The road marked closed
due to snow blockade I turn right to
it goes northeast the right
direction solitary
a thin road
among spare trees rough
macadam a watery sky something sadistic
intentional in how suddenly
one turn and white
floods in the background startled
my mind goes white white as in blind
rage as in white
fury aphasia exile in this state
where nothing is no one resembles
ugly unflattering pent-up
state of annulment
reached too soon
the snow blockade
and not enough just slick
glassy-eyed ice and the rubber wheels

I had wanted to feel solid blockage to
pound kick piss on round out with my fists
grind white on white rub frost
on frostbite some physical
body I could abandon
to

LANDSCAPE WITH MANTRA

I saw her at the hilltop
painting and it made me stop
suddenly tired perhaps it was the climb
she was surprised a little at my staring so
I went on crested looked back from the hill
rush hour light so delicate
in March in spring
magnolia forsythia plum cherry every kind
of bulb a runner made it breathless up and sank
to the ground head limp between his knees
and to the west the light
he could not see
me staring he just kneeled
hands stretched out to the sun
I thought of bedouins of dusk of prayer
in the alley where I stood between
him and the woman crosslegged
on her cushion still
filling in the white
words of her whitewalls words
no one spoke: *con*
corde concorde concorde concorde

ABSENCE OF NOISE PRESENCE OF SOUND

for Kim Stafford

The river's blue where it reflects the sky
brown where mountain flat out long
miles I know I drove them
here

Lean on them silent in the dust listen dry
particles lift to my nostrils
lips

Impossible to tell the silence from the breathing
insects lungs sagebrush breathing in
of winds I here grateful
to be trying

This a desire
not only in the mind
but how the muscle swivels
onto bone how heart wills the auricle
floods and its altered rate

The doorway with the mirror
appears
I have been warned

No wall no door no post no mirror
Still the same highway scooped out with a knife
still the same river
begin again
this time without choosing

I enter pretending it's a dream inscribed dust of dream
stroke stroke sign mountain name a name so excited I wake
myself who had been counting
on that

Oh the dream the moist the scaffolded prepared white wall
dream of a fresco

LANDSCAPE WITHOUT TOUCH

She has dreams of wolves it bewilders
her how it started with the skin
she put on totemlike one night
now she dreams whole packs and prowls
she prowls
her eye bright mica on the sidewalk
she prowls on bristling phosphorescent slight
she is somnolent by day
she sleeps in light
she becomes one
one less
one less human
one at home among wolves
one palest pelt
one

STILL LIFE

The spoon of desire is crusted
all of my lips are dry
are curiously
dry and warm as all
cold-blooded animals are
warm temperature that meets the air's
grows colder from the skin towards
the reptile center

Amphibian
I feel the air
warping a moist element
oceans of air around the lip
exquisite pink crenulated lip
talc-dusted bloodfilled underwater
lip so pure so
dry

LANDSCAPE WITH ANGELS

She slept she slept she blanketed
her five foot ten frame down with valium
the soggy gut-impacting down
and slept four days
and nights in a circle screaming
at the angels on their shining
bikes with their singing
chains real angels
real chains
the skull
of god emblazoned on
the dead hide on their backs she packed
herself in sleep
in disbelief
was it her father leaving
again at six at twentysix
her disbelief at pain that leaves
no bruise the pain of angels
leaving laughing
roars of metal engines chains
in the air like wings
beating and leaving
her unharmed by the police
report angels and devils
blue black choirs
of annunciation

PRAYER WITH MARTIAL STANCE

Days of eyes of eyes
nights of velocities
of insects planets soundwaves
of the brain
days and nights without interruption
green days of chlorophyl light and lungs
water and silence streaming
where no logger trucks
no biker rides I camp
here imagining this
daily discipline
of silence
Silence

Break in praise

Avoid causes of complaint

Change what you can't avoid

In this be

Ruthless

FAST

Since you've gone I've fasted having made the soup
whose recipe I sent (the mail
man came I wanted to
send something) cold curry thick with oranges
sweet clear onion underneath
the lid. The skin

of this truth's onion isn't
clear. Leathery obstinate I think
how boiled tongue peels simply how it is
the tastebuds (cellular abused by heat) that give
way to a larger muscle: tongue truth the matter of
taste and lack thereof the matter of

desire. Hear
me love. I'd do
anything and have to keep this in and you too anything
and have to keep from hearing. Is it complicity
that breeds contempt? Hypoglycemic
fasting for this sense

of desperation forcing me
thin as a needle without compass to let go
of hope and pray for clarity of mind of sky the cold
polar luminary any
finally cold clear star. Solstice
equinox solstice equinox nine months

without desire every time a reason why (ill
ness fatigue exposure trauma of old
love new love) all true
enough. Enough. I am not pushing

a friendship campaign like you said but love
intense unlimited perverse familial unpretentious

love
is it possible
that it is not enough? Without desire
in a field of stars the cold moon rising hungry
cold lip of a moon the pounding of my hungry
blood the starved

brain screaming *sugar* trembling
at last with clarity transparent lying
in the grass palms joined at the heart in love
desireless in prayer.

NAMĀSTE

Gary allow me
    I need to look up tonight
        to a desirable being

Three a.m.   The green
is very private at this hour   Shadowy
benevolence of trees the dripping shadow
rain of branches   Greater horizon
of tree and hill serene relieves
the eye   An artificial
drug they say induces
love for what appears
before the eyes   Consider a room
with an open window   One person touching
herself   Self
sufficience   In reference
to the substances inducing love the inner
eye is not mentioned   Four
a.m.   Alive
in a city I can walk
stiff-kneed and female feeling
safe   Night
air rare silence here
and there illuminated
glass   Head rests
easy   Infinitesimally
since summer letting down
of hair   No more a pretty
boy
      Deborah
           I'm grateful for this
limber body the Hatha
discipline your heart

which I see beating
equally
well in all you move   All
is important   The mouth makes O
O Praise
O Nothing   Deborah
we didn't know
when we agreed to love
ourselves well for a year
it takes just that to want to
understand
the task   Know
yourself   A Greek
man said that   (I tire
pointing out his mother too
said it proverbially as he
played in the dungy street
of the polis   I tire
of repetition
argument debate
of the obvious)   know
yourself he said and died
corrupting in such public ways
the youth   Another
Greek said anything
that appears and gives sensation
to exist is
real   Greek sounds harsh
and foreign to my ear   It pains me
to admit this of my mother
tongue and haven't
for years   The body guards
its limits   If I sprained my knee
today at final practice if I limp
towards you towards dawn

Deborah because I need and need to feel
my certain limits   Fallible
weak I have wept for this
Joy
          Olga-Maria told me
                    I would meet a man
of Saturnine
influence upon me   She told me
I was lesbian by some
mercurial venereal
and watery conjunction   Accidentally
she'd cast my chart for Stephen's
year that bull
headed junction of exact
day/time correlatives in May   Looking at mine
this time I wasn't
lesbian she said   She didn't mention
Gary   The Saturn
cycle you and I work
through   The planet Saturn
has been much maligned
informing us as it does of limitations calling
for concentration discipline
restraint of the mercurial
terrestrial the lovely
body   This body
          Deborah of work sprawled out
                    six months and nowhere
nowhere was the one
the old crone
wanted and grew white in heart
attack because I didn't
know it   In the dream
she revived
I think   A woman with a needle

jabbed and I
was loosening
her clothing   She had small young breasts like mine
Deborah like yours I've seen them
once as you were changing   Wanted
me to speak this
poem and I knew the one but not
by heart   I
        promised   Drove myself
                through Oregon
the greeny garden looking
for the heart felt heart
reviving drone   Daffodil
nasturtium narcissus lily
dahlia crocus hyacinth sweet names
of bulbs I do not have my heart in any
language   Friends
helping   *Magnolia*
one drawled *Remember*
me and the Dixie Dykes   I couldn't
lose magnolia all March   Profligate
indelicate lavender-hearted blossoms
face up side down in
any kind
of light   Day
dusk artificial   Other
flowers   *Did you wash*
your flower?   Does your flower
smell?   Don't play with your
flower   Mother
teaching me hygiene in
French in summer the
language the season of
love   Love
        Deborah what you say

39

                        you cannot
feel   Lust
passion pity aside respect
this love this friendly
flower   We don't
know the names of things
and still the body
presents us with its dreams   We speak
At breakfast we agree to love
our labor   Hard to keep
apart the work
from worker   Tried
to get around that
woman between me and my beloved
work for months   Gave
up learned to love   The sea
is more important than ever   Who can speak
of the irreducible   A house by the sea
is an honorable
goal in life   Deborah
I don't know if the old crone died
of waiting   Even if
this poem is
the one   Unspoken
healing
            You played flute
                        just out of hearing   Summer
and I too weak
to call   Shuttered and silence-hid
my weakness trapped me like a pack
of wolves traps sheep that will
not answer either
way to *do you*
want to
live?   You bought me talismans

and gifts   Handbound ten leaves
of numerology to teach
my numbers   Eleven you said
was incomplete   La Douloureuse   Eleven
widowed numbers   Migraine
splitting till I'd think
of dying   Not
really but you know
indulging
the mind   You the one I'd want
to call   I have never seen
your body   This cannot be
wrong   I've walked
shivering weak-kneed almost
to your door   In my heart
it is almost dawn   Trucks
stirring   Heading
home   If it feels like love
I told her who was terrorized and disbelieved it
is   I didn't read about three four
or five   I suspect that five is charmed
and sexy   Five fingers   The
Caritas   I'd planned
on seven (mystical
vibration of the body) but it was the time
for what love of the body appeared
palmed before the eyes   The two
crossed eyes   But nine
was union   Female
and male both (*principles*
in the margin) in
a perfect
form   She has a heart
        murmur   Perfect
                Lives

41

in Vermont   Green Mountain
states of the large
intelligence continuity
of land of being of love   I'm leaving
Oregon in April having lived through spring
once   Twice
in one year
to live through spring   Are there kinder laws
Deborah   Only to you
can I describe her
person   Person   A woman
I and thou like you in
herself   She opens
up she vanishes   She draws
her small tight very Jewish body close she dis
appears   Skinny
people often have
the heart
murmuring as if the blood
too close against the nap made sounds
a bloodsweet river   I've a hole
in my heart Deborah check it
every six months the doctor
said six years
ago
   I was hungry then
      for a woman   Lived in married
student housing she and I
illicitly on sublet couples
in the complex calling
us indulgently young
dykes   Lesbian?
I laughed one first fall night
Nothing to do with my
life   *Nothing   Always*

Lies   I lay twice that year
in student health erupting
hives   We never spent a night
in each other's bed   I had
as always in the past a single
mattress   Only last
          January up at dawn
                  the morning she was flying
to Vermont I woke
at home in my own double *having found*
in that language
in which I never loved
a woman *having found*
my person   Greek
blood flows through
my opened heart
less than sweet   I would like to see it also
perfect   The lesson
the lesson to be learned
murmurs close to the surfaces
of the body   She who disappears
Deborah is she who loves
her body   She enters
all doors opens all
windows on lookout for certain
fires   There are no mirrors
in her house no closets and
no key   There is
the garden
out uncurtained windows
knee-deep in snow   Flowers
have names not scents or colors
only   I want to know them
now because inside a dream
my sister said *They've taught me*

words for things I cannot feel   I fought
off evil
words for years tried to feel
her way   My sister was the one I dreamed
of saving   Across the ocean
from the parents—one who speaks
to me in a vocabulary
tentative of love he's never seen
in any dictionary one who speaks
to thank me for the flowers everything
I say to her
eyes is a flower   This too
is a limitation though like your
mother Deborah inert since adolescence
in asylums a
limitation not
solely of the body   If it doesn't feel
like love if it doesn't
feel...   Listen
he said to her who lies
for the moment's sake entirely
mutable her blood
incessant rising listen
the doctor said can you hear
where you can't hear it   There's evil
in the world Ramakrishna
says to thicken the
plot   I read that
          Gary
                    tonight as I was sitting
on the pot   I knew that would
please you pale
buttocked Gary in the moony night
playing practical jokes
on racoons   You spoke about the humorous

and other human uses
of manure the afternoon
I dreamed myself a path
away/towards
the garden path of praise
of silence and the wolves (I thought
them dogs then) licking
my neutral blood   It makes some sense
now Gary   I hope I remember
to look for it
again   Light   Still   Before
the dawn   Thin   Upright   Body
smarting still from the discipline   Hatha
Deborah you said means path
of concentrations   Circles
congenital around the hole
in my heart
       I cannot afford
            to enlarge
the temple   My
work is to confine
its size to force the holy back
into the flesh   I've looked
bright yellow eye
to eye and stood
among them now who prowl
intelligent indifferent warm
blooded round me   I will
I will stop to live
this
a desire
not only in the mind
but how the muscle swivels
onto bone how heart wills the auricle
floods and its altered rate   Pale slate

the sky the luminous
and iridescent bulbs   Medulla
oblongata   Wet
shoulderblades wet
cuffs skin-warmed familiar
rain   The beauty of the brain
Olga she wrote after she smashed the wind
shield with her own just narrowly
protected by a small hard
skull the beauty
of the brain is it creates
mistakenly whereas
the heart (learn to live
        with it) the heart
                indulges
in creation   Birds
too have names
in the many languages
I know   I recognize
by call
the crow   I heard birds call before
I saw the light the clarifying
light no longer dawn
of morning   To begin with
any one would do
of the senses   There are six
perceptible in all

March 1978

P. S.

How do you masturbate in Greek
you wrote around St. Valentine's I tried
listening to Keith Jarrett so exciting
to have some memorized I memorize
your letters same variety
of pleasure couldn't tell when
it was over had I come
or not not very
wet I'll come
I wrote in April dis
embodied disembodied
April All I love
is always being born
what I love is beginning
always Elytis sings in Greece
in mind in poetry I can begin
again not for poetry's
sake Jane poetry
fulfills you too
fulfill not every
time but over
time beginning over
poetry and you again this
way turn
your face this way
to the light how beautiful
you are

This book is designed by Tree
Swenson and Sam Hamill in
Deepdene type, which was de-
signed by Frederic W Goudy
in 1927 and named after his
estate at Marlboro. The cloth
edition, 150 copies, is letter-
pressed on Rives and signed by
the poet. The paper edition is
photo-offset from proofs of the
hand set type, Smythe sewn in
Neapolitan Blue Strathmore
Rhododendron covers with a
Telanian finish; the endsheet
stock is Tuscan, in Granite.